A Visit to the Doctor

by Anne O'Brien

illustrated by
Laurel Aiello

Harcourt

Orlando   Boston   Dallas   Chicago   San Diego

Visit *The Learning Site!*
www.harcourtschool.com

Welcome to the doctor's office. You are here for a check-up. You sit in the waiting room until they call your name.

A doctor's office is a busy place.
Other children are waiting, too. You
can read a magazine or talk until it is
your turn to see the doctor.

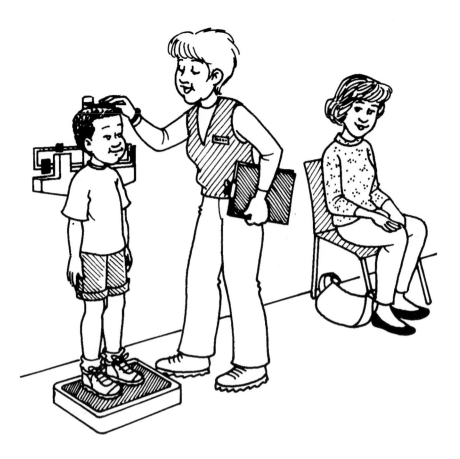

The nurse calls your name. You
follow her into another room. Your
mom comes, too. You stand on a
special scale. The nurse weighs you
and measures you.

The nurse writes down how much you weigh and how tall you are. Your chart shows your weight and height from your last visit. How many inches have you grown? How many pounds do you weigh?

Now it's time to check your blood pressure. The nurse puts a soft cuff on your arm. She squeezes a tube and the cuff puffs up. The cuff feels tight on your arm, but it doesn't hurt.

Sometimes the nurse needs to check your temperature. She puts a thermometer in your mouth. Don't talk! After a few moments, she takes it out and reads it. If you are sick, your temperature will be high.

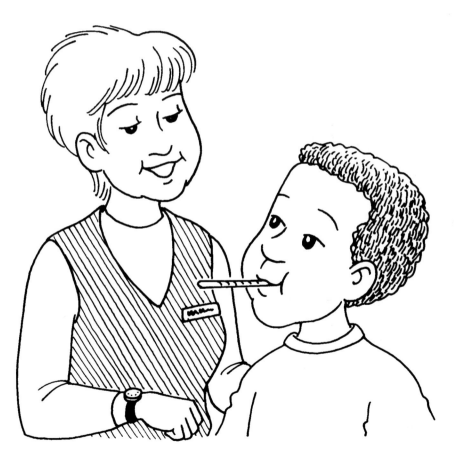

When the nurse leaves, the doctor comes in to check your health. The doctor asks you and your mom lots of questions. "How are you feeling? What do you like to eat? How do you like school?"

The doctor checks your eyes. She shines a light into each eye. "Look over here," the doctor says. "Now look over there."

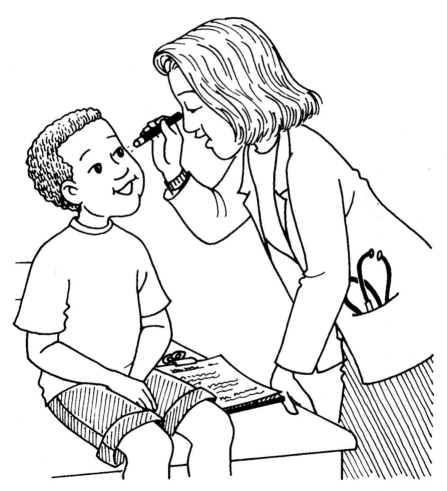

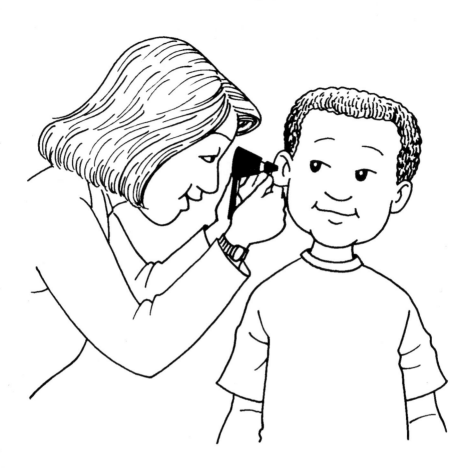

The doctor checks your ears. The
doctor uses a tool that can light up
the inside of your ear. She wants to
make sure you don't have an ear
infection.

The doctor checks your throat. She touches your tongue with a wooden stick. "Open wide and say, 'AHH!'" the doctor says. She looks for red spots in your mouth and throat.

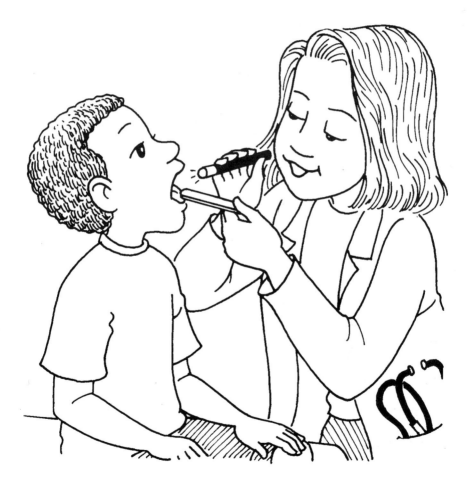

The doctor checks your knees. She taps each knee with a little hammer. Your foot goes flying up. Don't kick the doctor!

The doctor checks your heart. She
listens to your chest and your back
with a tool called a stethoscope. "Take
a deep breath," the doctor says. "Now
hold it." She listens carefully to your
heartbeat.

The doctor checks your legs. She watches you walk a few steps. Then she asks you to turn around and walk back. "What kind of sports do you like?" the doctor asks.

Your check-up is over! Everything about your visit is written down on your chart. If you ever get sick, the doctor can look up all the information about you.

The doctor and the nurse are glad you are healthy. They want you to stay healthy until your next visit. So you should eat healthy food and get plenty of sleep and exercise. See you at your next check-up!